STRIKE
THE SOT!

STRIKE THE SOT!

A Wizard of Id Collection
by Brant Parker and Johnny Hart

Andrews and McMeel
A Universal Press Syndicate Company
Kansas City • New York

8

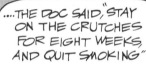

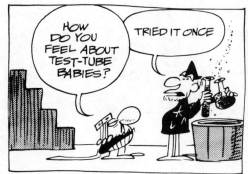

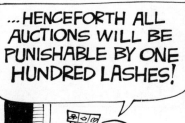

27

31

36

MADAM LAFRENZA WILL NOW ATTEMPT TO HIT FOUR OCTAVES ABOVE HIGH "C"

I TAKE IT, THE **MUTT** IS PART OF HER ACT

A LOT OF US FEEL THE ARMS LIMITATION DEAL WITH THE HUNS COULD LEAVE US UP THE CREEK WITHOUT A PADDLE.

PRESS CONF.

THAT'S NOT SO BAD...

WHAT DO YOU CONSIDER BAD?

BAD IS BEING **DOWN** THE CREEK WITHOUT A PADDLE.

PRESS CONF.

ELEVEN O'CLOCK AND ALL'S WELL

TWELVE O'CLOCK AND ALL'S WELL

THIRTEEN O'CLOCK AND ALL'S WELL

TELL THE CRIER TO BE IN MY OFFICE AT NINETEEN O'CLOCK IN THE MORNING

45

53

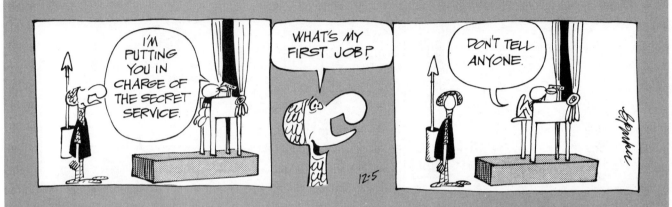

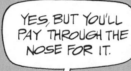

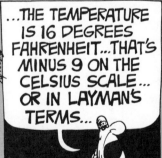

MY NAME IS SIR WALTER RALEIGH AND I'D LIKE TO BOOK PASSAGE ON THE NEXT BOAT TO THE COLONIES

12·3

SMOKING OR NON-SMOKING?

CAN I BEND YOUR EAR FOR A WHILE, FELLAH?

SURE, THAT'S WHAT BARTENDERS ARE FOR

12·4

....AS IT TURNS OUT, THE GUY USED TO FOLD TACOS FOR A LIVING

94

99

106

111

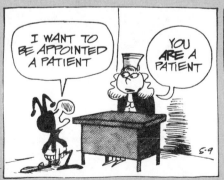

124